Introduc

GW00393631

A **little known 'walking' area**, the
unspoilt and very pastoral. There are
castles, waterfalls and large tracts of fores
Mountain or Carmarthen Fan is an easy d
of this dramatic and wild area. Llandovery is situated on the Heart of Wales
railway that runs from Swansea to Shrewsbury and this rail journey is one of
the finest in Wales. It is certainly worth taking a trip on the line and stopping
off at various points for walks or sightseeing. Another Kittiwake guide in this
series, 'Walks from the Heart of Wales Railway', is essential for this trip. Many
walks can be timed between trains. Llandovery is easily reached from the M4
in the south or via the A40 from the north and Brecon.

Whatever your level of fitness you will find, in these pages, walks to
suit all abilities and tastes. It is not uncommon to have the walks entirely to
yourself. Although an estimated time is given for each of the walks it is an
area of timeless beauty, an area where lingering and strolling are the norm.
Indeed I am sure that you will find the walks restful. They all follow rights
of way and have been individually checked. However, changes do occur. If
you find something that has changed please contact me via the publisher so
that the walk in question can be amended in future editions of this book. The
walks have been seldom walked and most paths are vague or do not appear
to be there on the ground. However, help is at hand as there are waymarks
in the form of posts or markers indicating the way. There is at least one walk
where Tir Gofal signs are prominent. This means that the farmer has come to
an agreement to allow people to follow a path across his land. Please respect
this to ensure continued access. If you have any doubt an enquiry to a nearby
house will usually be met with a helpful response.

Each walk has a map and description which enables you to follow
the walk without further help. However, on some of the more demanding
excursions, it is advisable to take a map and compass with you. Ensure that
you know how to navigate using these if the clouds roll down the mountains.
Take into account the weather and dress accordingly. Many of the walks cross
sheep farming land at some stage so you must keep your dog on a lead at all
times whilst walking these routes. Adhere to The Country Code, enjoy your
outings and have fun.

I would like to thank the Forestry Commission, and in particular Brian
Hanwell, for help and advice whilst compiling this book.

WALK I
Y PIGWN
in Roman footsteps

DESCRIPTION This is an interesting 2½ mile walk with great views the whole time. There are some extremely fine examples of Roman marxching camps as well as a couple of stone circles. One of these has 14 stones and is quite impressive. Allow 1½ hours.

START At the end of the tarmac road.

DIRECTIONS Follow the A40 from Llandovery towards Brecon as far as Trecastle. Turn right 200 metres past the speed restriction sign immediately beyond Trecastle Antiques. Drive up the hill out of the village past the de-restriction sign. Keep driving until a right turn gives access to a narrow and uneven tarmac road that ends at a gate. Drive through the gate and park immediately beyond it.

Follow the track straight ahead with constant views of The Black Mountain and glimpses of Usk Reservoir. After a mile or so beyond a short, almost imperceptible,

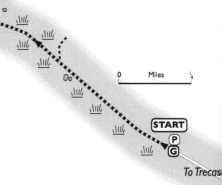

rise descend slightly into a hollow before the track starts to ascend again. At this point go right on a very narrow path that curves to your left and splits. Take the right hand branch to locate the two stone circles almost side by side. The right hand one has 14 stones whilst the left hand one has four. From the left hand circle go up to your left on a very narrow path then right on a more pronounced one to what appear to be grassy humps. *These are the Roman march-*

ing camps. Continue until just past them and turn up to your left by a metal post. Continue up through these 'camps' to the sedge adorned summit of Y Pigwn. Descend from here heading towards Usk Reservoir. Walk through more 'camps' to join the track. Turn left and follow it back to your car.

In AD 74 Julius Frontinus became governor of Britain for four years having succeeded Petillius Cerealis. During this time he is credited with having planned the Roman roads of Wales. Frontinus was a clever chap. He was a soldier, engineer and author. He wrote 'De aquis urbis Romae' (Concering the Waters of Rome) which detailed the history of the water supply for the city.

The Romans had established a fortress at Caerleon (Isca Silurum) to subdue the local people – the Silures. In summer manoeuvres during this process, marching camps were constructed by the Romans as overnight defences and were essential for protection against the fierce Silures. There is evidence of two camps on Y Pigwn. The construction is, typically, rectangular, 3 to 4 metres wide and about a metre high in front of which would have been a ditch about ½ metre deep. A camp of 8 hectares would accommodate one legion but the camp here is large enough to accommodate two. They would have camped in leather tents for a night or two before moving on.

2

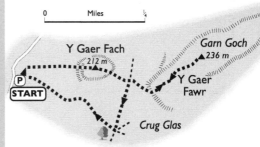

WALK 2

GARN GOCH

DESCRIPTION Although the walk is only 1½ miles there is plenty of interest along with some lovely views. Garn Goch is the largest Iron Age Hill Fort in Wales and the remains are quite impressive. To really appreciate the site, allow 45 minutes to an hour for your visit.

START From the small car park below the lower of the forts, Y Gaer Fach.

DIRECTIONS From Llandovery it is easiest to follow the A40 towards Llangadog for 6 miles or so to a roundabout where signs indicate the way to Llangadog and Bethlehem. Drive into Llangadog and through it following signs to Brynamman. A ¼ mile beyond the centre of Llangadog turn right over the bridge spanning the Afon Sawdde towards Bethlehem. Continue driving along the narrow road for 3 miles to the far end of the village where signs to Garn Goch indicate where you turn left. Turn right 400 metres further on where there is another sign for Garn Goch. This road is narrow and climbs steadily to a left turn after a mile. Take this turning, cross a cattle grid and park immediately on your left. There is an information board here.

Walk up the path left of the board. *This passes a large monolith commemorating Gwynfor 1912–2005 on the way to the summit of Y Gaer Fach.* From here there are great views of the main fort on Y Gaer Fawr. Keep on the path as it descends to the low point between the two summits. From here climb up to the top of Y Gaer Fawr bearing left at the pile of stones – an outlier for the fort. Walk along the level summit to the next pile of stones. Retrace your steps to the low point and turn left and walk down a shallow valley to the road. Turn right back to your car.

***T**he rock on Garn Goch – Red Cairn – dates from the Ordovician Period 495 – 433 million years ago. The Victorian geologist Charles Lapworth derived 'Ordovician' from the 'Ordovices' an iron age tribe of Central Wales whose name means 'the hammer fighters'.*

WALK 3

SUGAR LOAF
A mini mountain

DESCRIPTION Although this is a very short walk the views are well worth savouring from the superb vantage point above the road looking down the Tywi Valley. ½ mile, 20 minutes.

START At the car park and picnic site for the Sugar Loaf.

DIRECTIONS From Llandovery follow the A40 until just before Llandovery railway station and the level crossing – 'The Heart of Wales' line. Turn right on to the A483 towards Builth Wells. Follow this road until it starts to climb steeply and goes around two sharp bends. Picnic signs indicate that you turn right into the car park.

From the car park walk up the wide, closely cropped, grassy path up the hill. When the path eases off a broad, almost level ridge continues over the 329 metres high summit to the far end and viewpoint. Return the same way.

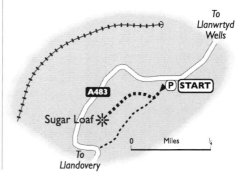

AROUND CARREG CENNEN CASTLE

DESCRIPTION This is a delightful 3½ mile walk. Good views of the castle, woodland, a variety of vegetation and an interesting cave entrance are just a few of the delights. The walk is well way marked by finger posts. Allow 2 hours.

START At the car park for Carreg Cennen Castle.

DIRECTIONS Follow the A40 from Llandovery towards Llandeilo. At the roundabout just before the town follow the A483 through it and continue to Ffarfach. At the far side of this village turn left at the roundabout – signed to Carreg Cennen Castle. Go under the railway bridge and turn right – again signed for the Castle. Turn left just as you enter Trap – another sign. Turn right at the next sign and then left again at the next and drive along the dead end road to enter the car park.

1 Walk out of the car park and turn right towards the farm. Walk past the shop and ticket office following the track towards the castle. Go through a gate and bear left up the path to the booth where your castle ticket is checked if you are visiting it. Go through the gate on your left and walk steeply down the path at first then more gently past several seats to a footbridge across a stream.

2 Go across this and follow the path up to a stile 50 metres further on. Go over this and continue to cross another footbridge. Continue up to another stile. Climb over this and follow the path between hedges to some steps and climb over a stile. Bear left to an uphill track as directed by a marker post. Follow the track up – there is a marker post by a right hand bend. Continue up the track to a junction. Go straight ahead – directed by a finger post – to where the track becomes a path. Keeping the fence on your right continue to a stile. *There is a superb view of the castle from here.* Go over the stile and follow the path up to a gate 50 metres further on.

3 Go through the gate and follow the path between fences to where it ends at a stile on the right. Climb over this. Turn to your right down a farm track climbing over a stile to the side of a gate almost immediately. Continue down the track and climb over a stile to the side of a gate to join a narrow minor road.

4 Turn right down the road and avoid the cattle grid by crossing the stile to the right side of it. Continue down the road for 300 metres to a gate on your right and a finger post. Cross the stile and bear half left across the field – *note how different the vegetation is here compared to the other side of the road.* Pass between two shake holes. Immediately beyond these go left over a stile by the finger post. Continue straight until the path goes half right and joins a track. Follow this down passing an old lime kiln – seen to your right – to a fenced enclosure. If you go over the stile you will come to the entrance to a cave – Llygad Llwchwr. CARE on the narrow path. Note the small entrance in the face. DO NOT ATTEMPT AN ENTRY.

5 Returning to the track climb over the stile and keeping the river to your left continue along the track to climb over a stile by a finger post. Go right to a cattle grid. Keeping on the track cross a stream, as indicated by a finger post. The crossing of this stream could be tricky after heavy rain. Keep following the track – there is a way mark on your left – and go past another finger post to pass through a gate by a cattle grid. Keep on the track – *where there is another great view of the castle, to a gate.* DO NOT go through this but bear left. Walk half right down the field, gently at first then much steeper, to a stile at the bottom right hand corner of the field. Climb over this and walk half left to a footbridge.

6 Cross this bridge that spans the Afon Cennen and walk up the path slightly to your right to a stile. Cross this and walk steeply up and right to a finger post and two stiles. Go over the right hand one. Walk half

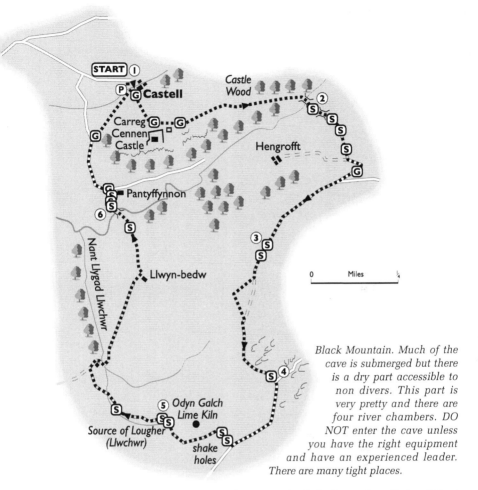

Black Mountain. Much of the cave is submerged but there is a dry part accessible to non divers. This part is very pretty and there are four river chambers. DO NOT enter the cave unless you have the right equipment and have an experienced leader. There are many tight places.

left up the field to the next finger post and through the gate to join a narrow tarmac road. Turn left up this and follow it to a kissing gate by a finger post. Go through the gate and walk across the field with the hedge to your right. At the top left hand corner of the field go through a gate that leads to the farm yard and shop. Turn left – or right if you want refreshment – back to the car park.

Llygad Llwchwr is one of the most important caves in the area. The resurgence is one of the largest in Wales. Water emerging here has travelled almost 5 miles in a straight line from where it went underground in The

A shake hole (properly called a doline) is where the roof of a cave passage below has collapsed leaving a funnel shaped depression on the surface. The vegetation around these is, as mentioned above, very different. The limestone where you are promotes good grass and ash trees whereas on the other side of the road you have walked down the harsh millstone grit supports sedges and bracken.

The lime kiln called Odyn Glach produced quicklime for making cement and for fertiliser for the fields. The limestone was excavated from the quarry directly behind the kiln.

LLYN Y FAN FACH

DESCRIPTION This pretty lake nestling under the dramatic cliffs of Picws Du has a wonderful legend associated with it. The walk can be curtailed at the lake by walking around it – 3 miles, or continued over Picws Du – 5 miles. This second option gives remarkable views from the grassy cliff edge looking down onto the lake. Allow 1½ hours if walking around the lake or 2½ hours if going over Picws Du.

START At a parking area by an information board beyond the tarmac road and Blaenau Farm.

DIRECTIONS From Llandovery turn up Waterloo Street where a sign indicates the way to Myddfai in 3 miles. Drive straight through Myddfai where a sign indicates the way to Llandeusant. Continue to a cross roads with the Red Pig pub on your right. Go straight across here. There is a sign pointing the way to Llyn y Fan. Continue to a 'T' junction and turn left, again signed to Llyn y Fan. Where the road ends a stony track goes straight ahead with a sign again indicating the way to Llyn y Fan. Follow this bumpy track past a farm on your right to a where the track goes down right over a cattle grid and through a gate into a level area. Keep going to the information board.

1 From the car parking area walk up the track past the information board to some buildings and a locked gate. Turn left on a signed path and follow it to rejoin the track again. Follow this up to a track junction. Keep right and walk up to the dam. There are two options here. Either walk around the lake for an easy day and return the same way back to your car or – and this is much better – follow instruction **2**:

2 From the lake bear right and follow a good, gradually ascending path away from the lake. *There are increasingly fine views down to the lake as height is gained.* The path levels when it reaches the broad ridge and then very gradually climbs over several undulations along the edge to the 749 metres high summit of Picws Du.

3 Leaving the summit the path descends, gradually at first but becoming very steep, to Bwlch Blaen-Twrch and a tiny stream. To your left, just before this, a narrow grassy path leads off. Follow this path under the cliffs of Picws Du. It becomes steep and descends around several steep hairpin bends to join up with another path at a 'T' junction. Turn left and follow a contouring path, with CARE initially, to where it descends. Keep a 'V' shaped gully to your right. Pass by a walled stream on your left and continue down keeping the gully to your right to reach a pool beside the track. Cross the outlet carefully – it is a slippery surface. Join the track and follow it back down to your car.

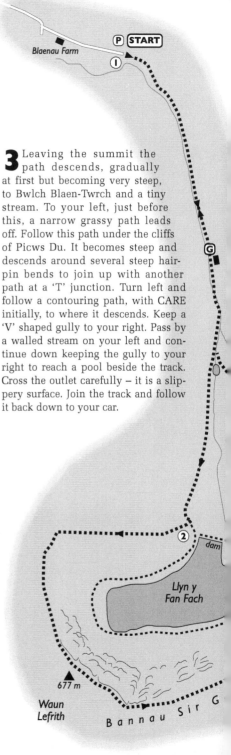

6

A **local young man**, the son of a widow from Blaen Sawdde near Llandeusnant, had agreed to marry a beautiful young maiden who had emerged from the lake. However, if he struck his wife three times she would disappear back into the lake. They were duly married. The maiden brought with her a dowry of some very special cattle that gave exceptionally fine milk. The couple remained very happy for many years in their house in Esgair Llaethdy, close to Myddfai, where they brought up a family. Over time the man did strike his wife three times, although unintentionally. According to the promise made the maiden disappeared back into the lake along with her cattle. On several occasions, though, she reappeared to help with the instruction of her children, especially Rhiwallon.

Llyn y Fan Fach

Eventually he and the other sons went to the court of Rhys Gryg from Deubarth becoming famous doctors who are known today as the 'Physicians of Myddfai'. Some of their medical formulas remain in Welsh manuscripts.

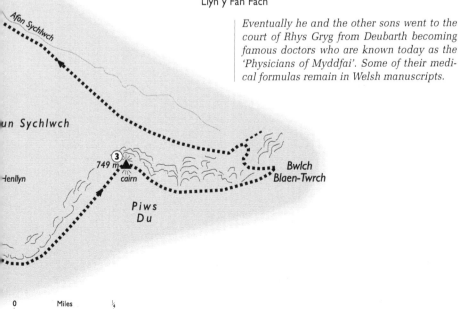

Afon Sychlwch

un Sychlwch

-lenllyn

749 m ③ cairn

Bwlch Blaen-Twrch

P i w s D u

0   Miles   ¼

AROUND USK RESERVOIR

DESCRIPTION This is a pretty upland stretch of water at an altitude of 320 metres, much favoured by fishermen. Views from several places towards The Black Mountain are tremendous, along with distant views of the Brecon Beacons. An alternative to the main walk avoids some of the forest track that this follows. Allow 3 hours for the 6 miles circuit.

START From the car park at the east end of the dam.

DIRECTIONS From Brecon take the A40 towards Llandovery. Drive to Trecastle and turn left from the main road onto the minor road in front of the Trecastle Antiques building. Follow this road uphill at first and continue, ignoring all turnings, to a junction below the dam. Turn left – a sign indicating Usk Reservoir is seen at this point – and drive over the bridge. Continue up the hill, to the left of the dam, to the car parking area on your right.

1 Walk from the car park up the road alongside the lake. The road deviates away from the lake to pass an Usk reservoir sign seen to your right by a track junction. Continue 300 metres further on the road to a junction with a forestry track going off to your right. This is marked clearly with two yellow topped green posts either side of the barrier. Follow this track. Ignore the junction to your right (signed 11 on your left) and walk to a left turn signed 12.

2 Follow this left hand track to the next junction – 13 – and bear right. Walk down and along the track to a 'T' junction and follow it to the head of the lake where a new footbridge avoids a ford! Keep walking along the track. It eventually joins another track. Bear right here. Continue along the track to a barrier and walk through the gate to the right of it. Continue along the track to the end of the dam. Walk across this back to your car.

ALTERNATIVE ROUTE

1 Start as for the parent walk but only as far as the Usk Reservoir sign. Turn right and walk down the track and go through a gate to reach the lake shore. The next 50 metres are subject to flooding in very high water! Keep walking along the track to where it ends at the lake edge.

2 Go up to your left here and walk to the left of a fenced enclosure. From the end of the fence go up to your left on a path to a yellow topped post. Continue ahead with a fence to your right. Where the fence ends continue walking ahead to reach a hide. From this there are great views of The Black Mountain. Keep following the path to reach another yellow topped post. Bear right to a very muddy track and follow it up to a gravel track. Turn left and walk up to a right turning signed 12 (see above). Continue your walk as in **2** above.

The north-eastern edge of the reservoir (marked A – B) is wheelchair passable – with care. This in itself is scenic as it goes along the edge of the reservoir. It is 2 miles there and back.

*T*he reservoir *is the most recent one to be built in the National Park. Building started in 1950 and took 5 years. It was inaugurated by Her Majesty, the Queen on the 6th August 1955. The 478 metres long and 33 metres high dam holds back some 2,700,000,000 gallons of water. A supply tunnel 2,370 yards long goes under Mynydd Myddfai to the Swansea watershed where a 10 mile long pipe line goes to the Bryngwyn Treatment Works 2 miles south-east of Llandeilo.*

Within the area there is a wide selection of flora and fauna. Red Kite are frequently seen and the Marsh Fritillary butterfly can be found here. The source of the River Usk is only a few miles upstream of the reservoir on Fan Foel. This reservoir has a reputation as one of the finest trout fisheries in Wales. The natural brown trout are supplemented by a regular restocking with rainbow trout.

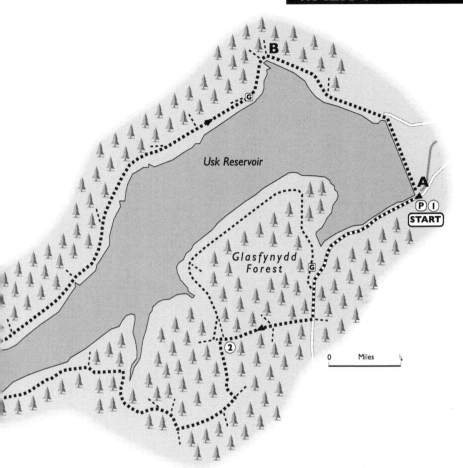

About the author, Des Marshall

Des has had a lifelong interest in mountaineering, climbing, walking, canyoning and caving. As well as being an advisor, trainer and assessor in outdoor activities, he has undertaken many expeditions worldwide but recently focused more on local excursions. Having lived in Machynlleth for many years he now lives in Utah, USA, visiting Wales frequently.

LLANDOVERY & THE AFON TYWI

DESCRIPTION Allow 2 hours for this pretty 3 mile walk that, initially, walks through the town of Llandovery before entering woodland. It then follows a lively stream and crosses farmland to reach the Afon Tywi. This is followed downstream back into town. The very many kissing gates make this an ideal walk for loved ones as the gates only open after kisses are made! Allow two kisses per gate!

START From the car park near the castle in the centre of Llandovery. There is a modest fee payable.

1 Walk out of the car park to the main road by the Tourist Information Centre. Turn right and go up the street to the road bridge spanning the Afon Bran. Cross over and follow a path by the side of the terraced houses, there is a marker post at the corner of the houses. Continue along a narrow tarmac path with the houses to your left to a kissing gate at its end. Bear right along the track with the river on your right to a path going off to the left below the next gate. DO NOT go through the gate. Follow the path with houses to your left and fence to your right. At a stile on your right turn left – DO NOT cross the stile – to reach a road. Turn right and follow it to a marker post. Follow the path to the right and walk along to a gate. Walk through this and pass to the right of a play area. Keep on this tarmac path to another gate. Go through this to join the A483.

2 Carefully cross the busy road and follow the minor road quite steeply uphill to St Mary's Church. Opposite the church on the other side of the road is a stile and a marker post. Cross the stile and head straight down the field to a hedge on your left. Continue to cross another stile and a further one 25 metres away. Walk up steps to the railway line. Cross over making sure there are no trains and walk down steps on the far side to a stile. Climb over this and go slightly left to

another, easily seen some 200 metres away. Cross over and continue walking straight ahead and away from a tiny stream on your left to yet another stile. Go over this and turn right to a gate. DO NOT go through this but walk down to your left for 10 metres to a stile with a way mark.

3 Step over the stile and follow the path alongside the stream on your left. Cross three short sections of boardwalk. Keep following the stream and fence to a footbridge with a way mark. Cross this and go over a stile to your left. Cross another footbridge 30 metres further on. Turn right, keeping the trees to your right, along the edge of the field towards the obvious gate. Cross the stile to the left where here is way mark. Go left with a fence and trees to your left and walk up to a marker post. Follow the track, ignoring the one going off to the left. Keep walking along the track to a stile by a gate with a way mark. Cross this and walk down the track for 50 metres to cross a stile on your left. Walk down the grassy path to yet another stile. Go over this to join a farm track. Go straight across this and go over another stile, with a way mark, to join a tarmac road. Turn left then almost immediately right. Walk up to Pont Dolauhirion.

4 Do not walk over the bridge but turn down left to cross a stile. Follow the bank of the Afon Tywi through three kissing gates. After passing through the third gate, situated above small rapids, follow the edge of the field round to another kissing gate on your right. Go through this and walk up a narrow path to the left of a stream. The path ends at a kissing gate by a narrow road. Follow the road and walk up to the stone bridge seen ahead with a wooden footbridge immediately beyond. Cross the footbridge and pass through another kissing gate. Keep to the edge of the field with a hedge on your right at first then a stone wall to, yes, another kissing gate. Go through this to join a narrow tarmac road. Cross straight over to go through another kissing gate with a way mark. Turn right and walk along the edge of the field with a fence and farm buildings to your right to the familiar sight of a kissing gate. If your

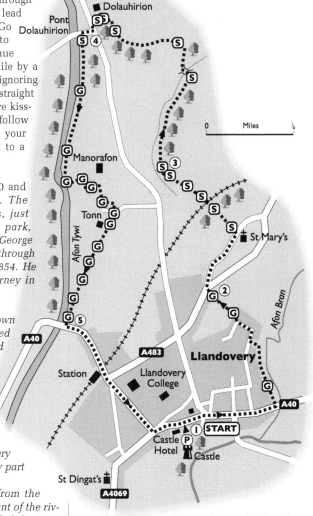

lips are not sore you will pass through this too and bearing right will lead you to a corrugated iron shed. Go through another kissing gate to the right of the shed and continue walking between fences to a stile by a gate. Climb over the stile and ignoring the gates to your left continue straight ahead passing through two more kissing gates. After the second one follow the path between the hedge on your left and a fence to your right to a final kiss at the last kissing gate

5 Go through to join the A40 and turn left back into town. *The Castle Hotel which you pass, just before you turn into the car park, was where the great traveller George Borrow stayed on his journey through Wales on the 9th November 1854. He recounted the story of his journey in his book 'Wild Wales'.*

***L**landovery is a medieval town and borough which received its charter in 1485 from Richard the 3rd. The famous Rhys Pritchard 1579 – 1644 was vicar of Llandovery who is particularly remembered for being the author of 'Ganwyll y Cymry' – The Welshman's Candle – a popular devotional work written in Welsh. Llandovery College was founded in the early part of the 19th century.*

Llandovery takes its name from the least worthy and very insignificant of the rivers that surround the town. Called the Nant Bawddwr – dirty water – it was diverted in 1836 through an arched culvert above which the street above paved.

The Town Hall was built in 1858. The actual council Chamber was situated directly above an open arcaded market. The former Market Hall, built in the 1840's has been renovated and now houses a craft centre atop of which is the town clock. At one time there was a tradition of clock making in the town.

Information on the Castle can be found on the information board below it in the car park.

***P**ont Dolauhirion was mentioned as the 'Bridge at Dolhir' in 1396. This was a timber structure and the bridge you see today was built in 1773. It has a span of 28 metres and cost £800 to build. The designer was William Edwards, a minister, stone mason and a self taught architect. He had become world famous for the bridge he had built at Pontypridd in 1750.*

WALK 8
LLWYNY-WORMWOOD

DESCRIPTION This 5 mile walk explores the hill and fine woodland above Llandovery. At the start of the walk there are some great views of the town. The walk mainly follows tracks which are linked by rights of way without any real paths, although there are waymarks. A good sense of direction is very useful. Allow 3 hours.
START From the car park near the castle in the centre of Llandovery. A modest fee is payable.

1 Walk out of the car park to the main road by the Tourist Information Centre. Turn right and walk up the street to Waterloo Street – signed to Myddfai – and turn right. Walk across the bridge spanning the Afon Bran and turn right 100 metres further on to Bronallt Farm. Continue down the access track to the farm. Go through a gate just before the buildings and go over a stile to the left of a gate where these end. Follow the track up into the wood. Continue to a gate and stile to your right just after you have started ascending. Go over the stile and follow the wide path/track up to a marker post on your left. Turn left, uphill, ignoring the track to the right. Keep walking up the track to a stile on your left to the right of a gate. This is at the edge of the wood.

2 Go over the waymarked stile and walk slightly right in the direction indicated. There is no path. Cross the field – *enjoying great views of Llandovery as height is gained* – going uphill to gain the highest point, where tyhere is a way mark. Bear right and walk down the same field keeping the fence to your left to a track and kissing gate to the left of a waymarked gate. Go through this and walk across the field as indicated – there is no path to another kissing gate right of a gate. There is a ruin and a wood to your left here. Go through the kissing gate and walk up the field with a fence to your

left (there is a very vague path) passing a small bulrush-lined pond to a fence corner. Continue in the same line up to a kissing gate. Pass through this and walk up the field keeping hawthorn trees to your right to reach a track. with a marker post on your right. Walk up the track to its top. Go over the stile on the left of the gate and go down the track for 40 metres. Turn right. Follow the path around to the right and continue between the gorse thickets on either side to enter a field. Bear slightly left away from the fence on your right to a marker post. Again there is no path! Just past another marker post there is a stile to the left of a gate. Go over this and follow the track between trees to a marker post on the left by a footbridge.

3 Do not go over the bridge but continue along the track and drop down to a stream. Cross this and go up to and over a stile left of a gate. Follow the track uphill and turn right at the track junction to a marker post at the next track junction. Turn very sharply left here and go up the track and through a wooden gate on the left just before entering the property of Cefn Rhuddan. *Once a ruin it is now a fine house.* DO NOT walk through the buildings of the property. Go through another gate and cross the field half right to the right hand far corner. Go through the waymarked gate to join a track. Cross straight over to a stile. Go over this and follow the track to a waymarked gater. DO NOT go through the gate but turn left and walk down to and over a stile. Walk half right with a fence on your right to a stile left of a gate. Pass this and keep the hedge on your left. Continue to a stile with another waymark, left of a gate and go over it. Walk right with the hedge on your right to a waymarked stile. Climb over this to enter an area of farm buildings. Follow the track through the farm and continue down the track to a waymarked junction. Turn left along the track ignoring the stile on your right 20 metres further leading down to a footbridge. Keep walking ahead on the track with the Afon Idw below to the right. Continue to enter Llwynywormwood by a gate.

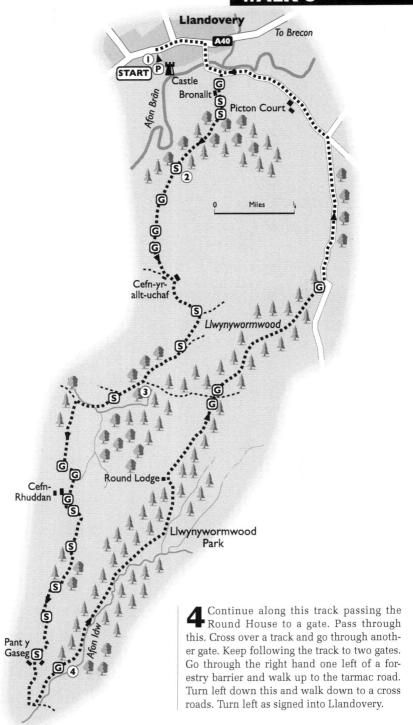

4 Continue along this track passing the Round House to a gate. Pass through this. Cross over a track and go through another gate. Keep following the track to two gates. Go through the right hand one left of a forestry barrier and walk up to the tarmac road. Turn left down this and walk down to a cross roads. Turn left as signed into Llandovery.

CIL-Y-CWM & MYNYDD MALLAEN

DESCRIPTION A 4 mile walk which explores the village and hills above this lovely village. There are some great views of the surrounding countryside. Some say that the view from Rhiw Cilgwyn above the high point of this walk is one of the best in Carmarthenshire. You can decide whether 'tis true or false. Look for the stone gutters, one of the endearing features of the village. A good sense of direction is very useful. Allow 2¾ hours.

START From your car in Cil-y-Cwm.

DIRECTIONS Follow the A483 from Llandovery towards Builth Wells for 400 metres to a zebra crossing. Turn left here. Follow the minor road under a railway bridge and continue for just over 2½ miles to a left turn signed to Cil-y-Cwm. Car parking is in the village on the roadside. Please park with consideration for the villagers and other road users on this narrow road.

I From your car, walk to the Neuadd Fawr Arms. This is almost opposite the Old Post Office, a lovely, old, but small terraced building. Opposite the Neuadd Fawr Arms there is a very well hidden way marker in a narrow lane indicating the way you need to follow. Turn left up this short narrow lane passing the Capel y Groes – *built in 1859* – and go through a gate into a field. Walk straight ahead to a stile and go over it. Continue in the same line to the next stile on the right reached by crossing a sleeper footbridge. Cross this stile and walk along the edge of the field with a fence and hedge on your left to the next stile which is crossed into another field. Go half right, as a vague path reveals itself, to another stile hidden from view at the top left hand corner of the field. Climb over this and another 30 metres further on. Continue over a footbridge and follow a sleeper bedded path with a fence to your left to a gap between fences.

Follow the path as indicated to the right to another stile. Cross this to enter a field. Go half left to a marker post just beyond a sleeper bridge and over a stile. Cross the field to a marker post and go over a stile right of a gate. Continue to a gate by a stone wall 100 metres further.

2 Go through the gate to the narrow tarmac road and turn left over a bridge. Follow the road up to a 'T' junction. Go sharp right to a waymarked gate on a track. Walk through the gate and follow the track up to a stile right of a gate. Go over this and continue up to two huge wooden gate posts. Walk through the gateway they form and up steeply to a gate. Go up the field with a fence to your left. Keep following the track through two more gates and then three more before reaching the col. (The ascent of Rhiw Cilgwyn goes off from here out to the left).

3 Go through the gate on your right, where signs indicate that there is no through road. True, there is no road, just paths for walkers. *There are superb views from the lower summit to your right.* Return to the col. Follow the path down on the right of a fence above young conifers overlooking Cwm Merchon. Continue down to a gate. Go through this and keep following the path down. Go left when it appears to split keeping the fence to your right and continue down to go through another waymarked gate. Walk half left down the pathless field to a waymarked gate. Go through the gate and go half right to join a track. Turn right.

4 At the next gate bear left. (The continuation of the obvious well maintained track beyond this gate is a private road. Please respect this). Follow this old Drovers Road to the farm buildings. Go through the gate ahead into the farmyard. Walk straight ahead between buildings to a gate at the end of the house. Go through this and then turn sharp left almost immediately and walk down the track to pass in front of another house. Continue down to a footbridge. Cross this to a waymarked kissing gate. Turn right along the narrow path to another kissing gate and walk half right up to the farm. Go

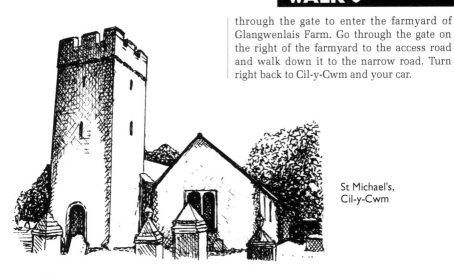

through the gate to enter the farmyard of Glangwenlais Farm. Go through the gate on the right of the farmyard to the access road and walk down it to the narrow road. Turn right back to Cil-y-Cwm and your car.

St Michael's,
Cil-y-Cwm

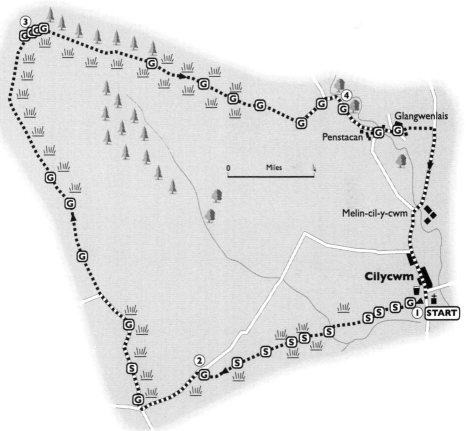

WALK 10
POOR MAN'S WOOD

DESCRIPTION This is a delightful 2¼ mile walk on the outskirts of Llandovery through a wonderful sessile oak wood. In spring there is a carpet of bluebells and wood anemones. Allow 1¼ hours.

START By a small quarry immediately after turning off the A40.

DIRECTIONS From Llandovery follow the A40 towards Brecon for a little over ½ mile and turn left opposite the caravan park and turning to Myddfai. DO NOT drive up the track to Dan-yr-Allt farm. Park by the quarry away from the track, as it is used by rather large tractors.

Dan-yr-allt Wood

Dan-yr-Allt

Llandovery

A40

START

P

Afon Gwydderig

Walk up the track to Dan-yr-Allt farm. Keep to the right of the buildings and follow the track up to a low marker post at a track junction. Go left and follow a grassy path between the hedge on your left and trees on your right. Continue to a kissing gate. Pass through this to a marker post and information board. Go left and continue with the fence to your left to the next marker post. Walk straight ahead to the left of the post. Continue to the next path junction and walk up to your right. This is quite steep. Keep going to where steps appear as the path curves right. A switchback leads up to where the path levels and starts to descend. Go down to a marker post and turn up to your left to a information panel. From here follow the level well defined path to where it descends. Keep walking down to the kissing gate of your outward walk. Go through the gate and retrace your steps back to your car.

WALK II

NANT MWYN LEAD MINE

DESCRIPTION This 2½ mile walk into the past glories of the area has some good views. The highlight of this walk is the extremely fine chimney which stands proud against the harsh backdrop of the old lead mine. The return walk along the quiet road is quite pretty. Allow 1¼ hours.

START From the Royal Oak Inn Rhandirmwyn.

DIRECTIONS Follow the A483 from Llandovery towards Builth Wells for 400 metres to a zebra crossing. Turn left here. Follow the minor road under a railway bridge and continue for 7 miles to the village of Rhandirmwyn. There is roadside parking but please do not hinder traffic. There is a shop, café and pub.

From your car, walk to the Royal Oak Inn and follow the dead end, steep road up to the right of it passing Pannau Street on your left, a very fine row of terraced cottages. Continue to where the road turns to the left. Straight in front of you there is a gate. Go through this. Follow the path up for 50 metres and turn left. Continue walking up the steep path through a dense conifer forest and pass through a gap in the fence. Keep going uphill as the path veers slightly to the right until a cairn on your left is reached by a track junction. Turn left down the track and continue bearing to the left, ignoring the right hand track, to a cross roads of tracks. Walk straight across and down into trees. *At the end of the trees you enter the mine area where there is a ruin and a very fine chimney.*

2 Follow the path across the spoil heap to a junction with a track. Turn left passing below the chimney to another junction where you again turn left, continuing down to the main access track. Walk down this and go through a gate to join the tarmac road. Turn left to return to Rhandirmwyn.

It is possible that the Romans mined lead here before the mineral was exploited again toward the end of the 1700s. Between 1775 and 1797 the mine employed 400 people and it is reported that 29,807 tons of lead was extracted during this period. The peak of production occurred in 1779 when a seam of lead 6 feet wide was found and more rich ground beside. In that year alone 2,500 tons were extracted giving a profit of £12,526. During the period 1835–1899 some 42,000 tons of ore were extracted along with 125 tons of 'brown' as the miners called zinc. At that time there were some 23 miles of levels, crosscuts and shafts. In the four months from June 1930, 165 tons of lead was extracted and 529 tons of zinc. The mine finally closed around 1932 because milling costs were too high.

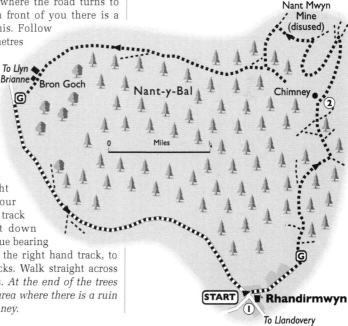

WALK 12
CWM RHAEADR

DESCRIPTION A pretty 3 mile walk in mixed deciduous and coniferous woodland, with an adventurous finale for those who want a little more spice in their walk. The waterfalls are situated in very dramatic surroundings. If sticking to the main route the walk is only 2½ miles. Allow 2 hours or 1½ hours for the regular walk. The walk is well signed with blue markers apart from the section up to the falls.

START From the Cwm Rhaeadr Forestry Commission car park.

DIRECTIONS Follow the A483 from Llandovery towards Builth Wells for 400 metres to a zebra crossing. Turn left here. Follow the minor road under a railway bridge and continue for just over 2½ miles to a left turn signed to Cil-y-Cwm. Drive through the village to a sign on your right indicating the car park to Cwm Rhaeadr is 50 metres further. Turn left into this car park and leave your car in the lower of the two parks. There is an information board here.

I Walk out of the car park by a finger post and a blue marker post up the path and continue to a path junction. There is a marker post here marked 39. Go straight ahead here and continue to a track. *Just before this on your right is a fine wooden carving of a horse. There is an information board at this junction.* Cross the track half left to a marker post and continue up to the next junction and turn right. At the next junction walk down the left hand path, firstly down, before walking up past a seat on your right close to a path junction. Turn up to your right. The path levels. Continue along past 2 seats and then descend slightly to a junction. Turn up to your right here – marker post 48 – to another path junction – marker post 38. Go left along the path to where it descends to a junction with a track – marker post 45. Walk left and follow the track down to marker post 66 on the left at the junction. Turn right

here along the track. Just after a huge pipe swallowing the stream a stile is seen to your right.

2 For adventurous people the walk up to the falls is well worth while. Whilst not difficult the path is exposed in places, narrow and has a tricky slippery crossing of the stream. This alternative will be impossible after heavy rain. Go over the stile and walk up keeping close to the fence on your left. At the fence corner turn right and follow the path to where it descends to the stream. Cross this slippery obstacle carefully to the far side. Continue up the narrow but not very steep scramble path to the base of the falls. An impressive spot. Retrace your steps back to the stile. Instead of climbing back up to the fence corner, follow the path alongside the stream to the stile and the track where you turn right along it. Follow the directions as in **3** below.

3 For those who do not wish to go up to the falls jump section 2. Continue walking along the track another 70 metres – marker post 91. Turn left down a grassy track. Keep following the path that becomes a track passing several marker posts and keeping the stream to your left. Keep walking down to a footbridge. Cross this and walk up to a track. Turn right along this to where the track bends to your right at a prominent junction with a path – marker post 29. Go up the quite steep path to marker post 39 seen earlier and turn right back to the car park.

A n all ability and barrier free trail goes off from the higher car park. Go up and left out of the car park and go up to a junction. Turn right to follow the gravely track in an anti clockwise direction for ¾ mile. It passes two pretty ponds and several picnic places. Allow 30 minutes for this.

The sculpture of the horse commemorates Henry Tudor who rode a horse bred in this area to the Battle of Bosworth. This is where he won the crown of England.

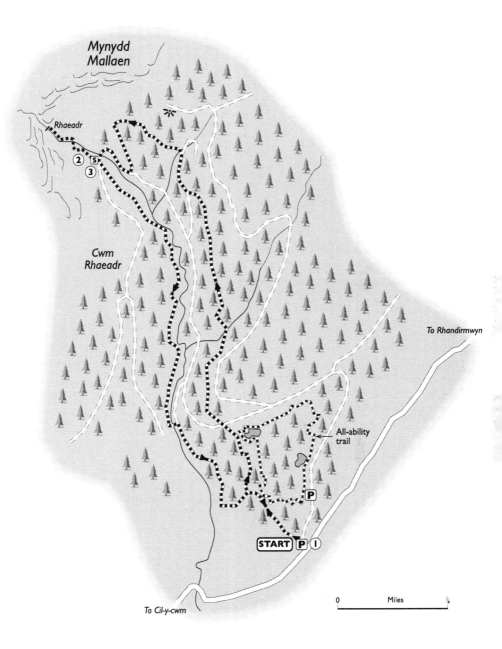

Mynydd
Mallaen

Rhaeadr

② Ⓢ
③

Cwm
Rhaeadr

To Rhandirmwyn

All-ability
trail

P

START P ①

To Cil-y-cwm

0   Miles   ¼

19

SOAR CHAPEL

DESCRIPTION This 2¼ mile walk explores the valley floor east of the lovely village of Cil-y-Cwm passing a short, but pretty section of the Afon Tywi just prior to Rhydwydd. Although the walking is easy a good sense of direction is very useful because there are no visible paths after section 2, although the way is very well way marked. Allow 1½ hours.

START From your car in Cil-y-Cwm.

DIRECTIONS Follow the A483 from Llandovery towards Builth Wells for 400 metres to a zebra crossing. Turn left here. Follow the minor road under a railway bridge and continue for just over 2½ miles to a left turn signed to Cil-y-Cwm. Car parking is in the village on the roadside. Please park with consideration for the villagers and other road users on this narrow road.

1 From your car, walk to the turning for Cynghordy. *Before you start your walk it is very worth while to look inside the little, medieval church close to the turning. It has a wonderful barrel ceiling.* Follow the quiet road towards Cynghordy. After half a mile you will reach a group of buildings on your left. One of these, Soar Chapel – *sometimes referred to as Tynewydd Chapel* – is quite old. Continue down the road until you reach the road bridge over the Afon Tywi.

2 Do not cross the bridge but go through a wooden kissing gate on your right and go up to the track – there is a Tir Gofal sign at the kissing gate. Follow this with the Afon Tywi for company to your left. Continue to Rhydwydd Farm passing Tir Gofal signs on your left. At the farm walk through a red painted gate to the right of the buildings of Tir Gofal sign – and walk by the right hand side of the farmhouse along a concrete track. Keep following this between fences as it curves right around the top edge of a field.

3 When the concrete ends go to your left through a gate to Tir Gofal. Walk up to your left with a fence on your left to a rickety iron gate. Go through this, and, keeping the fence to your right, continue to another rickety gate. Pass through this and keep walking until you see a gate up to your right. Go through this with a way marker on the far side which is almost hidden. Walk half left down the field to a gate. Go through this. Continue to your left through the next gate and turn right for 20 metres to another gate with a Tir Gofal sign. Abergwenlais farm is to your left.

4 DO NOT go through this but follow the track to the right to where it goes straight ahead into a field and another track bends to your right after going through a gate with a Tir Gofal sign. Following this track you walk through another gate. From here walk slightly left up the field to two gates – marked Tir Gofal – either side of a track. Go through these and continue across the next field half left to another gate, again marked Tir Gofal. Go through this and walk slightly left across a field to go through a gate on the left. Continue to a stile marked Tir Gofal. Cross this and walk around two sides of the field, first right then left – DO NOT walk across the field – always keeping the hedge to your right. At a stile go over and walk ahead along edge of field to a gate on the right.

5 Go through this and walk up the field with the Afon Gwenlais on your left to a gap in the wall ahead. Step over the slab to join the narrow road of your outward journey. Turn left back to your car in the village.

S oar Chapel was built in 1740 but rebuilt in 1786. It was, possibly, the earliest Methodist Chapel in Wales. Wales most famous hymn writer, William Williams, 1717–1791, was a life long member. He was a local man and perhaps his most famous hymn was 'Arglwydd arwain trwy'r anialwch' (Guide me O Thou Great Redeemer). The area around Cil-y-Cwm, Caio and Llandovery became known as the 'Bro'r Emynwyr' – the hymn writers area.

Soar Chapel

Close to Abergwenlais Farm there are two 'Burnt Mounds' by the track. These crescent shaped mounds of burnt stone and charcoal date back to the Bronze Age and were possibly cooking places.

Hidden behind the church and overlooking the Afon Gwenlais is Ysgoldy Fach. This small schoolhouse was one of Griffith Jones's Welsh Circulating schools in the 18th century.

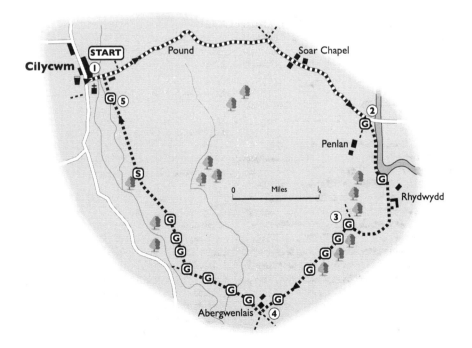

THE CIRCUIT OF CWM RHAEADR

DESCRIPTION This is superb high level 3¾ mile walk above the cwm with some extremely fine views. Well worth seeking out. The elusive view of the waterfall comes towards the end of the walk. *Please note that this circuit will be impossible to complete following or during heavy rain.* Allow 2¼ hours.

START From the Cwm Rhaeadr Forestry Commission car park.

DIRECTIONS Follow the A483 from Llandovery towards Builth Wells for 400 metres to a zebra crossing. Turn left here. Follow the minor road under a railway bridge and continue for just over 2½ miles to a left turn signed to Cil-y-Cwm. Drive through the village to a sign on your right indicating the car park to Cwm Rhaeadr is 50 metres further. Turn left into this car park and park in the lower of the two parks. There is an information board here.

1 Walk out of the car park and turn right down the road, around a double bend and past some white terraced cottages on your right. Continue a further 200 metres to where an obvious farm track goes right. Turn right but do not follow the track rightwards. Go through the gate in front of you and follow a grassy track. Keep following this track as it rises walking between fences to a stile left of a gate. Go over the stile or through the gate into open country.

2 Bear very slightly right and follow the path between bracken up the hillside to join a track. Go right and up to a grassy track. Follow this as it rises steadily. *Great views develop as height is gained.* Just before rocky outcrops bear right along well defined sheep tracks that gradually ascend. When

these level out bear right keeping the steep downward slope to your right in sight. Keep following well defined sheep paths until you are opposite a very prominent path seen to your right on the other side of the stream valley. Trend right towards this picking up another defined sheep path that leads to a 'washpool'. Good landmarks here are the substantial blocks of rock at stream level.

3 Cross the stream (this will be impossible after or during heavy rain). Go up the path on the far side. After 200 metres or so head out to your right to the edge of the very steep slope – *for magnificent views of the cwm.* Follow this edge up along intermittent sheep paths that lead to a better, more pronounced path. Keep walking close to the edge to where the path starts to descend. Walk down keeping on the better path, to the left of the forest on your right, to a gate on your right close to an enclosure.

4 Turn right through the gate to a mountain bike track. Go straight across this and follow a track down to a forest road. Turn right and walk up this for 250 metres for a view of the waterfall. *A convenient commemorative seat is welcome and a good spot to have lunch.* Return to where you joined the road and turn right down another track to a 'T' junction. Turn left. Walk down to a blue marker post – numbered 48. Turn up the path to your left and follow it to a path junction. Go left (blue marker post on your right number 68) to another junction where there is an information board on the right. Turn right along the path and go left again at the next junction (number 20). At a forest road junction go half left, cross the road and walk to the left of an information board. (Marker post 85). In 20 metres you will pass a wooden carving of a horse on your left (see **Walk 11** for information about this). Continue straight ahead at the next junction number 38) back to the car park.

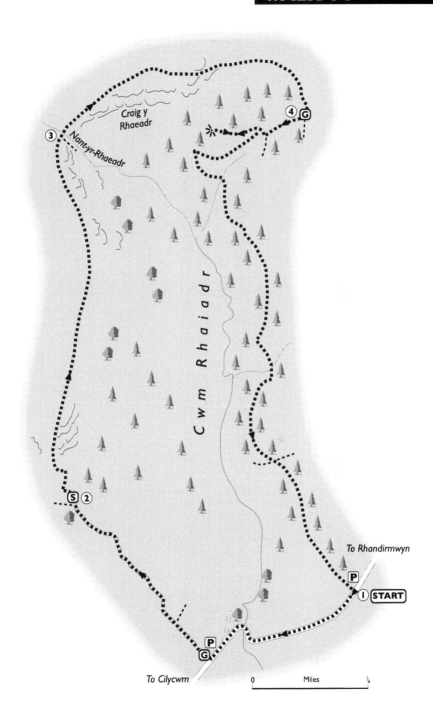

Craig y
Rhaeadr

Nant-yr-Rhaeadr

③

④ Ⓖ

C w m   R h a i a d r

Ⓢ ②

To Rhandirmwyn

Ⓟ

Ⓘ START

Ⓟ
Ⓖ

To Cilycwm

0   Miles   ¼

COTHI VALLEY & CAIO

DESCRIPTION There are some great views of the Cothi valley and surrounding countryside on this 7½ mile walk. It travels through an estate, follows the Afon Cothi and enters the upland above the valley before going through a forest to descend into Caio, a charming and pretty village with an ancient church. Allow 3½ hours.

START From Dolaucothi gold mine.

DIRECTIONS Follow the A40 from Llandovery towards Llandeilo. Turn right in Llanwrda and follow the A482 towards Lampeter. There are also signs for the Dolaucothi gold mine. Keep following signs for the gold mine turning right before the village of Pumsaint. Drive to the car park on your right for the mine.

1 Walk out of the car park to the road. Cross straight over and through a gate into the Dolaucothi Estate where there is a sign for the estate walk. Follow the manicured path to the river. The path turns right so follow it above the river. Continue through a gate, or over the stile, and turn left. Walk down to a bridge over the Afon Cothi. At the far side of the bridge go through a gate and turn right along a wide farm track. Continue to a marker post and gate on your left. Go through the gate and over the stile just beyond. Follow the path towards a high stone wall and take the path to the left of it. There is a marker post by the side of the wall. Continue to a stile. Cross this and walk up steps, indicated by a way mark and marker post, to join a farm track. Turn left as waymarked to another marker post at a track junction 100 metres ahead. Follow this track bearing right to another track junction.

2 Turn right and walk along the track ignoring a marker post and gate on your left (this is another walk not described in this book). Keep following the track passing a track going off to your right. Cross over a stile on your right 200 metres beyond. Walk half left across the field to the far right hand corner and climb over a stile. There is a waymark on the far side. Bear right to the fence. Go up the edge of the field with the fence on your right and over another stile. There is a waymark on the far side. Keeping the hedge to your left continue to where it ends and turns left. You continue straight ahead to a marker post. Follow the track through an avenue of trees and climb over a stile to the side of a gate where it ends. There is a way mark at the far side. Follow the narrow path to the right of the fence to another stile 100 metres further with a waymark on far side. The path is now level and is followed via a slight rise to join a track. Turn right down this and climb over a stile to the right a gate. Continue to the metal footbridge. Cross this and the stile at its end. Go right to pass through a gate and up to a stile 50 metres further. Cross this and walk very steeply up to another stile.

3 Climb over this to join a narrow tarmac road. Turn right and follow it down to a road junction. Turn and walk along this road. The hill up to your left along here – Allt Dinbeth – is the possible site of an Iron Age fort. Keep walking along the road to a track going off on your right. It is signed for Glan Meddyg. Turn right up this track and follow it uphill to a right hand bend. (A gate straight ahead gives access to the end of the Roman aqueduct). The walk continues around the bend and uphill to the farm. Go through a waymarked gate and follow the track keeping the buildings to your left to a marker post by a right hand bend. Keep on the track and walk up to a gate. Go through this and three more. After the third gate bear slightly left to a gate.

4 Go through this to enter the forest. Follow the good track down for a mile keeping straight ahead at all junctions until a picnic table is seen close to the river on your left. Walk past this keeping it to your right and continue to a footbridge. Walk up the far side to a junction with a track. Turn right along this and bear right at the next junction to join a narrow tarmac road. Follow this

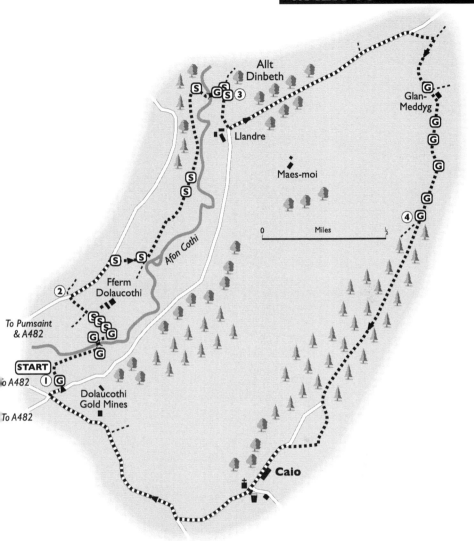

into the very pretty village of Caio. Walk past the Brunant Arms, *perhaps having called in for refreshment first,* and continue along the road passing the school up to your right. At the road junction turn right and walk up the fairly steep road. Continue along it back to your car at Dolaucothi gold mine. Here you may wish to do the tour of the mine.

*T**he** quite large church in the village of Caio dates back to the early medieval times. On the outside north wall there is a Christian monument dating back to the 6th or 7th century.*

*A**fon Cothi** is an important spawning ground for Trout and Salmon. To get here they have travelled some 20 miles upstream from the Afon Tywi. They lay their eggs in the gravel beds that are 40 miles or more from the sea.*

MASONRY AT ITS BEST: CYNGHORDY VIADUCT

DESCRIPTION This 2¾ mile walk starts off by crossing the 'Heart of Wales' railway line before continuing across farmland. It then descends to the valley floor and continues beneath the finely constructed Cynghordy Viaduct. Continuing, the walk follows a very quiet road back to the start. It is possible to extend the walk but includes a section of narrow and very busy main road and is not recommended. Allow 1½ hours.

START Near Cynghordy Railway Station.

DIRECTIONS Follow the A483 from Llandovery towards Builth Wells. Pass the right turning to Tirabad on a sweeping left hand bend and continue another 400 metres to where a sign indicates the left turn to Cynghordy. Drive along this road following signs to the station. At the right turn to it the road becomes rough and gravely. Although there is limited parking alongside the track it is best to park close to the junction with it. *PLEASE DO NOT block the track as this is the access road to the station for rail users.*

1 Walk up towards the station. Just before reaching it turn left up to a level crossing. Climb over the stile listen for trains. If all is clear cross over and climb over a stile on the far side. Follow the track up to a way marker on your left just before the track bends right to Dildre. Go straight ahead as indicated, to the left of a huge shed, through the gate and walk up and across the field by a line of trees up to your right. Continue through a gateway. *Strangely there is no gate and the right gate post has a fence attached to it but not the left!* Walk down the field half left to a gate. Go through the gate and down the track for 20 metres. Turn sharp left to pass through a very rickety iron gate. Bear right and cross a footbridge into a field – all

this is very overgrown. Walk up the field with the fence on your right to a stile at the top corner right hand corner. Go over this stile to join a track

2 Cross the track and walk diagonally right across the quite swampy field – take CARE here – to a hidden gate with a waymark, just to the right of the left hand top corner of the field. Go through the gate, cross the stream and walk up to your right on a poor track keeping the fence to your right to a marker post. Continue ahead across boggy ground to a gap in the fence. Turn left before the gap and walk up the field with the fence to your right – *good views unfold as height is gained.* At the top of the field there is a gate. Go through this and walk between fences. This is quite awkward due to the tall sedges and grass but continue to a rusting gate. Go through this and walk down the field and through the next gate still continuing down to reach a stile with a waymark on your right. Climb over the stile to enter the grounds of Pen Lan. Bear right to cross another stile and walk along the boundary of the property to your left to join a track. Follow this track down crossing over the Afon Bran before going through a gate to join the road.

3 Turn right along the road and walk beneath the superb Cynghordy Viaduct. Continue along the road passing a chapel on your left just beyond the viaduct to a bridge over the river. A track goes off left before the bridge but you will walk over the bridge and follow this quiet and quite pretty road going straight on at a 'T' junction back into Cynghordy.

Trains finally crossed Cynghordy Viaduct when it was finally opened in 1868 after many delays during the construction process, not least the unsound foundations that had to be replaced. The cost for building was £15,610 11s 6p (£1,234,135.30 at today's prices). The length of the viaduct is 258 metres and there are 18 arches each with a span of 31 metres. The highest of which is over 30 metres high.

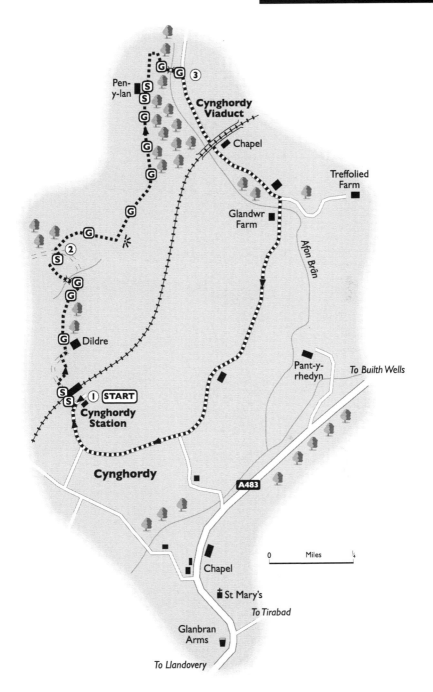

Pen-y-lan

③

**Cynghordy
Viaduct**

◆ Chapel

**Treffolied
Farm**

**Glandwr
Farm**

Afon Brân

②

■ Dildre

**Pant-y-
rhedyn**

To Builth Wells

① START

**Cynghordy
Station**

Cynghordy

A483

Chapel

St Mary's

To Tirabad

**Glanbran
Arms**

To Llandovery

0   Miles   ¼

AROUND DINAS
and a visit to
Twm Sion Cati's cave

DESCRIPTION This is a gentle 1½ miles walk through lovely woodland. Part of the walk follows the infant Afon Tywi, a marvellous stretch of river having many cataracts and fast flowing water. Allow 1 hour.

START At a lay-by off the minor road leading to Llyn Brianne.

DIRECTIONS Follow the A483 from Llandovery towards Builth Wells for 400 metres to a zebra crossing. Turn left here. Follow the minor road under a railway bridge and continue for 10 miles to where there is a lay-by on the left hand side of the road, at the edge of a wood, immediately beyond a tiny stream. There is also a very old railway goods van close by.

1 A stile is seen up to your left. Walk up to it and climb over. A more pronounced path is joined 20 metres further on. Turn left and continue past some seats on your left. Keep walking along the level path to a point high above the Afon Tywi. Follow the undulating path below some crags but remaining high above the river until a fast flowing and tumbling tributary is met: this is the infant Tywi. The left hand branch is the Afon Pysgotwr Fawr.

2 Follow the undulating path above the steeply descending river, *which has some very fine cascades*, to a large boulder blocking the path. Go up to your right immediately before it on some rough stone steps. *(From here a direct ascent up the steep hillside leads you to Twm Sion Catti's cave. Regrettably there is much graffiti here, although some dates back to 1830).* Back on the path, continue ahead still above the tumbling river to where the path rises at a wooden staircase. Go up this and continue up some rougher steps to the top of a small rise. Drop down slightly to a seat. From here follow the path in a narrow ravine almost beside the noisy river. A metal handrail helps

you over a slippery rock step. Keep walking close to the river to another short flight of steps. Go up these and some more a little further. Steps then descend to a grassy area with some alder trees. There is another seat here! The path continues alongside the Afon Tywi. THIS IS IMPASSABLE WHEN THE WATER IS HIGH. Keep going past a seat to where the path starts to rise and leaves the river. Pass a rustic seat on your left and continue to a wooden boardwalk.

3 Turn right, upslope, here and follow the right hand path at a junction. Continue along this level path through oak trees back to your car.

The Afon Tywi, at 68 miles long, is the longest river flowing wholly in Wales. The source is high up in the Elan Valley hills close to Crug Gynon some 451 metres above sea level. It flows into, and then out of, Llyn Brianne to reach the sea just below Carmarthen.

Llyn Brianne, a storage reservoir, was created during 1971–72 at a cost of £5.7 million by the West Glamorgan Water Board. Water is supplied to an area stretching from Kidwelly to the outskirts of Cardiff. It takes its name from the tiny stream of Nant Brianne which joins the Afon Tywi close to the dam. Although it was deemed a favourable site opposition was strong but not successful in the attempt to stop the construction. Many old farms were submerged. The rock-filled dam is 91 metres high and retains 63,300,000 cubic metres of water. Llyn Brianne Power Station was opened in 1997 by Richard Page MP and Iain Evans the Chairman of Hyder plc. It generates enough electricity to supply the annual needs of 6,500 homes.

Twm Sion Cati can be presumed to be the Welsh version of 'Robin Hood' and the cave here was his legendary hideout. His anglicised name is Thomas (Twm) Jones (Sion). Cati was his mother's given name. Born in 1530, he died in 1620. In his later years Twm was given a Royal Pardon for his thievery and became a Justice of the Peace as well as a Welsh historian.

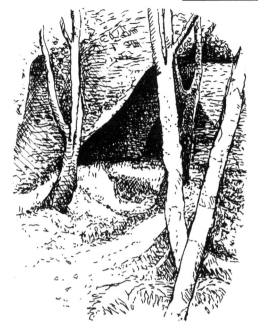

Twm Sion Cati's cave

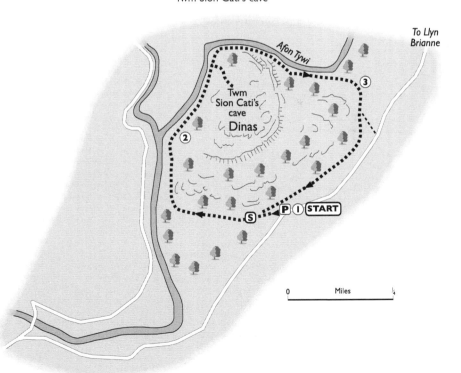

WALK 18
CAPEL CARMEL

DESCRIPTION This 4½ mile scenic walk explores the upland and valley farmland mainly by following tracks. The steep bit comes right at the end, walking back up the road to your car. There are some great views of the surrounding countryside, the upper Cothi valley whilst to the north the church tower at Caio can be seen. Allow 1¾ hours.

START Capel Carmel on a rough track.

DIRECTIONS Follow the A483 from Llandovery towards Llandeilo. Turn right on to the B4302 where it is signed to Talley Abbey just before the roundabout close to the town. Continue driving to Talley. Immediately past the speed restriction sign turn right. *TAKE CARE – this junction is not signed.* There is a bus shelter on your right just after you have turned. Follow the narrow road bearing left at the first road junction – signed to Carmel. A rough track on your right before the chapel is wide enough for cars to be parked BUT parking is limited. Please park with care and be sure to allow access for farm vehicles using the track.

1 Walk back along the road you have just driven and turn right down the dead end road. Follow this to a marker post where the tarmac ends. Bear right along the track and follow it down gently. After a short rise go through a gate and walk half right with a fence on your right along the track to a gate by a marker post. Go through the gate and continue with the fence to your right and go over a stile left of a gate. Turn left and keeping the fence to your left continue to a telegraph pole with a way marker. There is also an iron hurdle here. Go right to join a track. Continue down this track, where there is a waymark on your left by another hurdle, to a stile to the right of gate.

2 DO NOT go through the gate or over the stile. Continue straight ahead down the field to the fence. Turn right and to follow it keeping it to your left to reach a stile to the left of a waymarked gate. Climb over. There

is a glimpse of Lower Talley Lake here. Walk down the field with the fence on your left to cross another waymarked stile to join a track.

3 Turn right over the cattle grid and follow the track along – ignoring the right hand track beyond a gate – to Gwynion Llethri farm. Keep to the left of the buildings. At the semi circular roofed barn, where there is

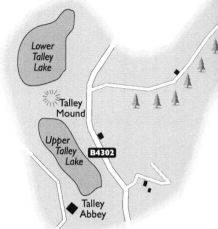

a waymark, walk to the right of it. Continue along the track to go through a waymarked gate, and another just before Garreg Lwyd.

4 Keeping the house to your right walk through the yard and then bear left to a gate. Go through this and walk straight ahead. *There is a metal map of the immediate area hanging from a tree here!* Bear right over slightly swampy ground to pass between two marker posts and cross a footbridge into a field. Walk around the edge of this keeping the fence to your right and walk up to a stile right of a waymarked gate. Go over the stile and up the field with trees to your left and a fence to your right to a gate on the right. Go over the stile to the right as waymarked. Follow the track up into a field and keep walking straight ahead with a hedge to your left to a gate. Go over the waymarked stile to the right and join the tarmac road. Turn right and follow it back to your car at Carmel.

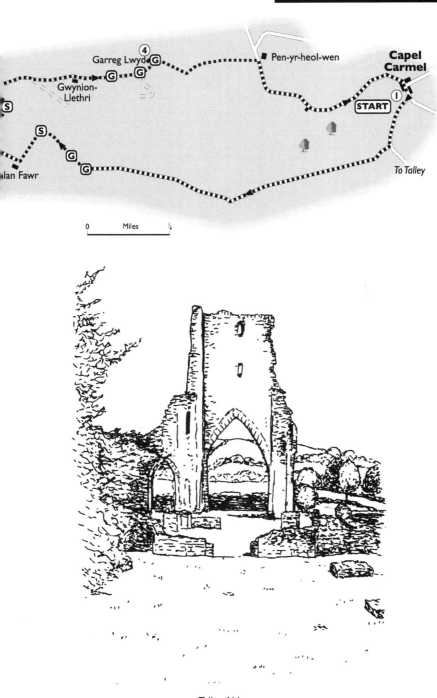

Garreg Lwyd ④

Pen-yr-heol-wen

Capel Carmel

Gwynion-Llethri

START

①

To Talley

Ⓢ

Ⓢ

lan Fawr

0   Miles   ¼

Talley Abbey

WALK 19

CWRT Y CADNO & THE UPPER COTHI VALLEY

DESCRIPTION There are some fine views of the upper Cothi valley and down the valley on this 4¼ miles walk. It travels through good grazing land and towards the end of the walk the faint remnants of a Roman Aqueduct can be seen to your right. Allow 2¼ hours.

START From the large car park close to Cwrt Methodist Chapel.

DIRECTIONS Follow the A40 from Llandovery towards Llandeilo. Turn right in Llanwrda and follow the A482 towards Lampeter. There are also signs for the Dolaucothi gold mine. Keep following signs for the gold mine turning right before the village of Pumsaint. Drive past the entrance to the mine. Keep following the narrow road to Cwrt-y-cadno and the large car park on the right immediately before the chapel.

I Walk up to the chapel. Turn right down the road immediately beyond it. Cross the bridge spanning the infant Afon Cothi and up the hill on the far side. Where the road bends left turn right up a track. Almost immediately turn left where there is a sign for Troedyrhiw Nawpont. Walk up this track and through a waymarked gate. Go up to a marker post by the house. Keep left keeping the house to your right and pass through a another waymarked gate. Walk to your right up the field keeping the fence to your right to a marker post where the fence bends right. Go right here to join a steep track. Turn left up this and follow it steeply, keeping the fence to your right, and continue up to a marker post by a gate. Keep walking up the field, still with the fence to your right, to another waymarked gate on your right at the top of the field. Go through the gate and keeping closely to the fence on your left join a prominent track by a waymark. Follow this up to two gates. Go through the left hand one. Walk straight ahead keeping the fence on your right. The next gate is blocked off, so step left. Continue up in the same line to another gate. Pass through this to rejoin the track and follow it up until almost level with the top of the forest on your left.

2 Bear right across the field to a gate with a plastic lid marker. Go through this gate and follow vague tracks straight ahead. The track fades and even more vague tracks trend slightly rightwards over to Cefn yr Bryn. A better marked path is found and followed to the left just below the summit of Cefn yr Bryn. It then bears right across an area of sedges and continues towards a gate seen ahead to reach a track. Walk to your right down this to a gate. (You have realised that the gate you were walking towards was being used as a guide and not the one you are now going to go through!) Go through the gate and follow the track down for 200 metres or so and then leave it to walk down a grassy ridged section of field to join another track. This is 100 metres to the right of the fence. Walk down to and over a stile.

3 Continue ahead at first then bear left along an improving track to a gate. Climb over wooden bars to the right and follow the well marked grassy track to a gate on the right, just before two gates ahead. Go through this right hand one of these and bear right to pass through another gate. Follow the track along and then down. Pass through a gate just after starting down and continue your descent through two more waymarked gates. *Before going through this last gate there are the remains of a Roman Aqueduct to your right.* Having gone through the gate, turn right at the track junction and follow it down to join the tarmac road. Turn right along it back to your car.

Cwrt-y-cadno

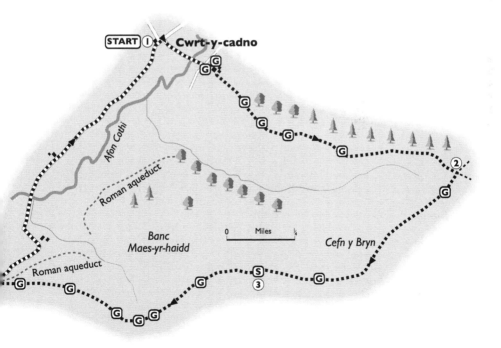

AROUND PEN Y DINAS & THE AFON IRFON

DESCRIPTION This is a pretty 4½ miles walk after the initial forestry tracks. A very steep descent just after these demands care but there are some lovely valley views and some fine woodland. An exciting *alternative* crossing the Afon Irfon adds to the fun but only when water levels are low. Allow 2¼ hours.

START Llanwrtyd Church.

DIRECTIONS Follow the A40 from Llandovery towards Brecon as far as Llanwrtyd Wells. Drive over the bridge spanning the Afon Irfon and turn left. Continue along the minor road which crosses back over the Irfon. Continue straight ahead, when the road bears right, to reach Llanwrtyd Church.

1 Walk up the tarmac road to your left above the car park to Dinas. Where the tarmac ends follow the track as it curves around Pen y Dinas to a track junction. Go steeply up the track to your right to reach a large turning area. To your left is a gate. After you have passed through this into a field, turn right and follow the fence to your right to the edge of the wood. Go over the stile into it and follow a very steep path down, CARE, to where it levels. Turn left along an old, level forest track to where it joins a main forest road. Go to your right and continue to the barrier. Walk around this to join the valley road.

2 Turn left and walk up the valley to reach Pwllgolchu (Washpool) – *a fine but small waterfall in a lovely stretch of river.* Continue walking up the road to Penybont Uchaf. Turn right where there is a bridleway finger post. Go through a gate and across the Irfon to another gate. Continue to where you see a way marker on a large, old gatepost. Keep to the right of the house and bear right

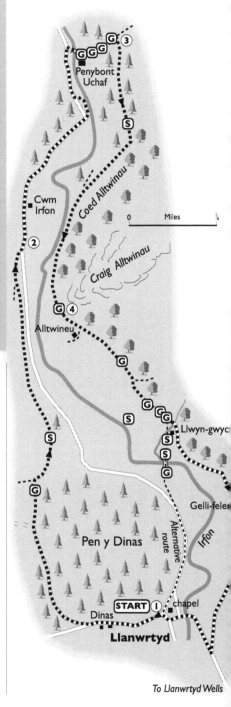

34

through the buildings to pass through two gates to enter a sloping field. After a sort section of track a marker post indicates where you turn up to your left to follow a line of marker posts up the field. At the top of the field go through a gate and turn right up the obvious path.

3 Continue through the larch forest to where it ends. A short rise up to your left leads to a stile. Cross the stile and tiny stream just after to reach a marker post. Go down to the next marker post 20 metres away. Follow the path down to a fence, where there is a waymark. Keeping the fence to your right follow it down and go through a gap in fences. The path continues down with the fence and forest now to your left. Continue to join a track at a waymark. Turn left along the track and follow it through a gate and on to join the tarmac road close to Alltwineu.

4 Turn left up the road and follow it through a gate. The road continues through a fine sessile oak wood. Ignore the track going up to your left and keep following the road through two gates to reach Llwyngwychwydd farm. Follow the track through the farm keeping the house to your left to rejoin the tarmac. Follow this past Gellifelen and go through a gate. Continue to a road junction. Turn right and walk to the next road junction and turn acutely to your right. Follow the road over the bridge spanning the Afon Irfon back to your car at Llanwrtyd Church.

4 ALTERNATIVE Opposite the Llwyngwychwydd farm house go through a gate and another to enter a field. Walk half left across the field to a stile into another field. Cross this and another stile and continue to the river edge. In LOW water stepping stones stand clear. Cross these to the far side of the Afon Irfon to join a track. Follow this up through a gate to join the road. Turn left down the road back to Llanwrtyd Church.

WALK 21
AFON IRFON
ALL ABILITY TRAIL

DESCRIPTION This is a pretty ¾ mile walk by the side of the tumbling Afon Irfon and through some fine woodland. The trail follows the red markers. Allow ½ hour. The red and blue trail combined is a mile so allow ½ hour for this one too.

START Pwll Bo car park.

DIRECTIONS Follow the A483 from Llandovery towards Brecon as far as Llanwrtyd Wells. Drive over the bridge spanning the Afon Irfon and turn left. Follow the road up the valley for a little over 3 miles, then cross the Afon Irfon into the spacious Pwll Bo car park on your right. (There is another similarly named car park further upstream).

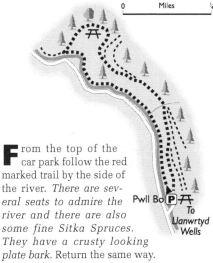

F rom the top of the car park follow the red marked trail by the side of the river. *There are several seats to admire the river and there are also some fine Sitka Spruces. They have a crusty looking plate bark.* Return the same way.

For a different way back for the more able, follow the blue markers up to your right when the hard surface ends and follow the quiet forest track around. Go through a gate that leads back into the car park.

There is a very fine but small waterfall below the road bridge that you cross when driving into the car park. The best view is obtained by walking downstream a short distance to view this fall.

35

TWO CASTLES:
one very old,
another just old

DESCRIPTION An interesting 4¼ mile walk that has glimpses of the Afon Tywi, two very different styles of castle and some pretty woodland and lots of bluebells in springtime. Allow 2½ hours for the walk plus plenty of exploring and visiting time.

START From the main car park in the centre of Llandeilo.

DIRECTIONS From Llandovery follow the A40 into Llandeilo and follow signs to the main car park on your left in the centre of town. A modest fee is payable.

1 From the top right hand side of the car park walk out to the main street under an arch by an information board. Turn left along the main street and walk past the Castle Inn and St Teilo's Church. Cross the road and walk down to where you follow a raised flagged footpath past some very pretty cottages. This path leads you naturally to where you turn right before the bridge along a dead end road that quickly becomes gravel. The Afon Tywi is on your left. Go through a kissing gate on the right and follow the track. *There is an information board on your right, indicating you have entered Castle Woods Nature Reserve.* Continue along the track to where it splits. Walk to your left down a path that leads to the derelict looking Llandyfeisant Chruch.

2 Follow the path around the church to the right and go down to a gate. Go through this and turn up to your right for 10 metres to another gate. Follow the fence on your left to a gate where two fences converge. Go through the gate and go left to another 30 metres further on. Pass through this and follow the path up through the wood to another gate. Walk through this to a track and turn left along it keeping the fence on your left. Continue to where a gate by a seat is seen on your left. Go through this and walk gradu-

ally up through the wood. The path levels off – *there are glimpses of the Afon Tywi below* – and leads to a track. Turn left along this and walk gradually up to some information boards on your left. Continue to the old Dinefwr Castle. There are commanding views of the Tywi Valley from here. Leave time to explore.

3 Exit the castle and walk back down the track. Some 50 metres past the point where you joined the track from the path turn left. There is a marker post opposite this turning for people coming the opposite way and directing them to the castle. There is also a seat and a large tree stump here. Walk gradually down passing an information board to a gate. *Lots of bluebells here in May.* Go through this and enter open parkland. Keep to your right alongside a fence and follow a gravel path down to a large and small gate. Go through the smaller and continue up the well maintained track passing the old slaughter house on the way to the National Trust car park.

4 Walk down the main entrance drive after visiting the 'new' castle for ½ mile to a wooden gate on your right. Go through this and follow a good track down and past an interesting vertical rock formation. Continue down to where a gate gives access to Llandyfeisant Church. Turn up to your left here to the right of a tiny stream to steps leading to a footbridge. Go up more steps at the far side and follow the path around to join a tarmac road. Turn right along this to the fine entry gateposts for the park. Turn right and, keeping straight ahead, walk into town. Turn left when you reach the main street and return to the car park and you car.

L landeilo dates back to the 6th century when it was a known Christian centre. Towards the close of that century one of the main Christian figures of Welsh history at that time, St Teilo established his base here. He has several churches dedicated to him around South Wales as well as in Brittany. It is well worth looking around the church for much more information.

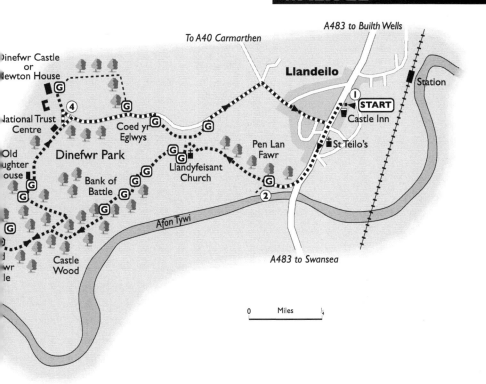

Because 'Old' Dinefwr Castle commanded such great views of the surrounding countryside it was probably used as hill fort by the Romans. However, the first mention of a castle here is recorded in the Book of Llandaff in the 7th century. Protection from marauding Vikings was needed, so the castle was built by Rhodri Fawr around 850 AD. When Rhodri died he split Wales into three kingdoms. Deheubarth, the southern, was administered from here by Hywel Dda one of Wales' most renowned leaders. When the Normans continued their expansionism into Wales in 1067, Dinefwr declined in importance. Rhys ap Gruffydd began a struggle for independence in 1135 after the death of Henry the Fifth. He regained the land captured by the Normans as well independence for Wales. Rhys was a great patron of the arts staging the first National Eisteddfod at Cardigan Castle in 1176. He died in 1197. His sons then vied for control with Rhys Grug coming out on top. He sacked the town of Swansea,

took over control of other castles and died in battle. That great Prince Llewelyn ap Iorwerth rose to power and came to Dinefwr. Other changes took place until Edward the First captured Dinefwr in 1277. It was never to be returned to the Welsh, even withstanding Owain Glyndwr's rebellion in 1403! It was finally abandoned by the Rhys family around 1600. The castle was only opened to the public in 1998 after restoration work.

'New' Dinefwr or Newton House is thought to date back to 1603 although there has been a Newton House here since about 1430. There was much alteration over the years even to the extent of that extraordinary landscape architect Capability Brown putting in ideas that were not taken up. The castle was used as a casualty clearing station during the 2nd world war. Lord Dinefwr sold the house in the late 1970s when it fell into disrepair. It was finally taken over by the National Trust in 1990, when restoration work commenced.

37

TALLEY HEIGHTS

DESCRIPTION This 2½ mile walk explores the woodland and farmland above this lovely old village. There are some great views of the surrounding countryside and to the Upper Talley Lake below. The Abbey is well worth looking round either before, or after, your walk. There are toilets just beyond the start. Allow 1¼ hours.

START From the little car park by the Abbey.

DIRECTIONS Follow the A483 from Llandovery towards Llandeilo. Turn right on to the B4302 where it is signed to Talley Abbey just before the roundabout close to the town. Continue driving to the village and the little car park for the Abbey.

I Walk up the road passing some toilets and a turning up to Talley Wood on your left. Continue up the road for 200 metres and turn left up a waymarked footpath. Upper Talley Lake is on your right. Zigzag through the barrier and continue up the quite steep path through the wood. At a junction with a track keep walking straight ahead as waymarked, up the path to another junction with a track. Follow this up and left, ignoring the stile on the right, rising all the time past an almost hidden picnic table 20 metres away to your right where there are commanding views of the surrounding countryside. Keep walking up the track to where it levels and another picnic table, this time to your left. After a slight drop there are two gates 100 metres further. Go over the stile on your right as waymarked.

2 Cross the field keeping the fence and conifer wood to your left to reach a stile in the corner. Cross this, there are two waymarks, and step left to walk down a small grassy cutting with a fence to your left to another stile just after a tiny waymarked footbridge. Go over the stile and bear left still with the fence to your left. When the fence turns left walk straight ahead as way-

marked to a gate on your left. DO NOT go through this. Walk downhill with a fence to your left passing by the ruins of Blaen Cwm yr Efail. There is a marker post 20 metres to the right of the fence here. Walk ahead from the post with a line of trees to your left to another marker post. Bear slightly left here to the corner of the field and a stile. Climb over this and walk half right across the field to another stile and way marker. Go half left across the field – *there are great views* – to two stiles 10 metres apart. Cross these, being careful of the ditch between, and walk right to another stile.

3 Cross this and follow the path with a fence to your left. This quickly veers away from the fence and continues down past two marker posts. The path then becomes steeper as it descends through the wood. Bear left at a marker post and continue along a level section to cross over a stile. Keep following the path through a mature wood to join a track. Go right and continue down around a left hand bend to marker posts on your left and right. Walk to your right here down the path to a gate. Walk easily around this! Keep following the wide track down and around a right hand hairpin bend, where there is a marker post. Keep walking down to a 'T' junction, where there is another marker post. Turn sharp left. Follow the track to a very minor tarmac road. Turn left along this and continue to another 'T' junction where you turn left back to your car.

The name of the Abbey and village – Talyllychau – is derived from the lakes Upper and Lower Talley Lakes (the 'Head of the Lakes'). Formed at the end of the last Ice Age the lower lake is now a nature reserve. The canal linking the two lakes was installed by the Edwinsford family and the mound between the lakes is that of a motte and bailey castle.

Talley Abbey had its foundation in the 12th century and the striking remnant of the tower dates to this period. It was founded by Lord Rhys ap Gruffydd of Deheubarth. Edward I assigned it to the care of the English Premonstratensian Abbeys. During the Middle Ages the Abbey became neglected and

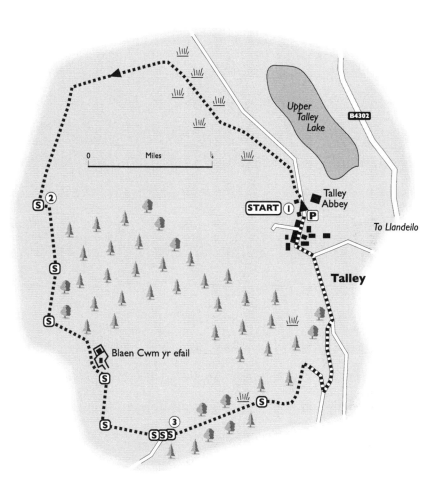

Upper
Talley
Lake

B4302

Talley
Abbey

START ①

P

To Llandeilo

Talley

Blaen Cwm yr efail

③

0   Miles   ¼

was closed by Henry VIII. He also confiscated all its estates. As time went by, even though it was used as a Parish Church, it became very ruined. A new Parish Church was built in 1773 using stone from the Abbey. It was patronised by the Williamses of Edwinsford. This 'new' church still has the original 18th century box pews. Each one is numbered and graded for the Edwinsford family, retainers and tenants.

PRONUNCIATION

These basic points should help non-Welsh speakers

Welsh	English equivalent
c	always hard, as in cat
ch	as on the Scottish word loch
dd	as 'th' in then
f	as 'f in of
ff	as 'ff in off
g	always hard as in got
ll	no real equivalent. It is like 'th' in then, but with an 'L' sound added to it, giving 'thlan' for the pronunciation of the Welsh 'Llan'.

In Welsh the accent usually falls on the last-but-one syllable of a word.

KEY TO THE MAPS

———	Main road
═══	Minor road
●▶●	Walk route and direction
①	Walk instruction
– – –	Path
∿	River/stream
Ⓖ	Gate
Ⓢ	Stile
△	Summit
🌲🌳	Woods
🍺	Pub
Ⓟ	Parking

THE COUNTRYSIDE CODE

- Be safe – plan ahead and follow any signs

- Leave gates and property as you find them

- Protect plants and animals, and take your litter home

- Keep dogs under close control

- Consider other people

The CroW Act 2000, implemented throughout Wales in May 2005, introduced new legal rights of access for walkers to designated open country, predominantly mountain, moor, heath or down, plus all registered common land. This access can be subject to restrictions and closure for land management or safety reasons for up to 28 days a year.

Published by
Kittiwake
3 Glantwymyn Village Workshops, Glantwymyn, Machynlleth, Montgomeryshire SY20 8LY

© Text & map research: Des Marshall 2011
© Maps & illustrations: Kittiwake 2011

Drawings by Morag Perrott

Cover photos: *Main* – The Cothi Valley, Des Marshall. *Inset* – St Michael's, Talley, David Perrott

Printed by MWL, Pontypool.

ISBN: **978 1902302 93 5**

Care has been taken to be accurate. However neither the author nor the publisher can accept responsibility for any errors which may appear, or their consequences. If you are in any doubt about access, check before you proceed.